Age of Discovery

500 Interesting Facts About the European Exploration
During the Early Modern Period

Welcome Aboard, Check Out This Limited-Time Free Bonus!

Ahoy, reader! Welcome to the Ahoy Publications family, and thanks for snagging a copy of this book! Since you've chosen to join us on this journey, we'd like to offer you something special.

Check out the link below for a FREE e-book filled with delightful facts about American History.

But that's not all - you'll also have access to our exclusive email list with even more free e-books and insider knowledge. Well, what are ye waiting for? Click the link below to join and set sail toward exciting adventures in American History.

Access your bonus here: https://ahoypublications.com/

Or, Scan the QR code!

Table of Contents

Introduction

Exploration and discovery have shaped the world we live in today. From the **Portuguese exploration of Africa** in 1415 to **Captain James Cook's voyage to New Zealand** in 1769, these brave explorers took monumental steps toward uncovering new lands and cultures that would forever alter world history. In this book, you will take a journey back through time as we explore some of the most important expeditions.

We'll start with Portugal's adventures into unknown waters beginning in 1415 when they set out to **discover an African** trade route around Cape Bojador. With **Christopher Columbus's** famous voyages across the Atlantic Ocean to India just over fifty years later, it was clear there were no limits to what could be explored if one dared to try.

Privateers also took part during this era by engaging pirates and taking on more nefarious tasks while exploring the distant coasts of Asia, Africa, and America. These activities helped shape the slave trade industry, which was in existence for centuries.

We'll also explore many more famous explorations, such as **Jacques Cartier's journey** down the Saint Lawrence River, **Spanish colonization in Mexico and Peru, the French exploration of Canada,** and **the Dutch exploration of Indonesia.**

Finally, we will look at some more modern expeditions, including **Captain James Cook's voyage around New Zealand** in 1769, **the Russian exploration** of the Aleutian Islands in the 1670s, and **British expansion into North America** between 1700 and 1763.

So, join us on this incredible journey through time to discover what these explorers accomplished during their daring adventures.

Portuguese Exploration of Africa
(1415–1488)

This chapter will explore the incredible history of Portuguese exploration in Africa between the years 1415 and 1488. Discover some fascinating facts about the intrepid explorers, such as their discoveries, achievements, and impact on world trade.

1. In the early 15th century, **the Portuguese began to explore Africa** by sailing down the West African coast in search of a sea route to Asia.

2. In 1434, **they successfully rounded Cape Bojador** and continued southward along the West African coast.

3. **The Portuguese explorers reached as far south as present-day Angola** and made contact with local kingdoms there.

4. By the end of the 15th century, **Portugal had established trading posts** and fortifications on the West African coast, such as Elmina, where a very successful gold mine was located.

5. In the 1440s and 1450s, **Prince Henry "the Navigator"** was an important figure in the Portuguese exploration of the northwestern coast of Africa.

6. **In the mid-15th century, the gold trade between Europeans,** primarily the Portuguese, and the Ghanaian people started.

7. In the 1450s, **Portuguese explorers reached Cape Cross and the southern tip of present-day Angola.**

8. By 1471, Portugal had established settlements at **Sofala** (Mozambique), **Kilwa** (Tanzania), and **Mombasa** (Kenya).

9. From 1482 to 1483, **Diogo Cão sailed south** along the west-central African coast.

10. In 1484, he arrived at **the mouth of the Congo River** and sailed up the river, becoming **the first European to explore** considerable parts of west-central Africa.

11. In the late 15th century, **Portugal began its conquest** to gain control over larger parts of the coastal regions, including territories around Cape Bojador and Cape Agulhas.

12. On January 17th, 1501, **explorer João da Nova sighted Ascension Island and Saint Helena;** he named the former after the day of the discovery.

13. **Explorer Bartolomeu Dias was the first European to round the Cape of Good Hope in Africa** on January 11th, 1488.

14. On March 12th, 1488, **explorer Bartolomeu Dias became the first Westerner to see the Indian Ocean** from the southern tip of Africa when he arrived at Kwaaihoek near Mossel Bay, South Africa.

15. **Vasco da Gama set sail from Lisbon to India** on July 8th, 1497, reaching India by circling around the African continent in 1499 and marking a new era in trade between Europe and Asia.

Alvise Cadamosto's Voyage around the Coast of Africa (1454)

This chapter **will explore the remarkable journey of Alvise Cadamosto, an Italian explorer** and trader who set sail in 1455. We'll take a look at interesting facts about his voyage around the coast of Africa on behalf of Portugal.

16. **Alvise Cadamosto was an Italian explorer and trader** who is known for his exploration of the African coast in the mid-15th century.

17. **Born into a merchant family in Venice,** he gained a lot of experience on the seas during his early years, being a member of several different **Venetian missions** before he set sail around the coast of Africa.

18. **Sponsored by Portugal's Prince Henry the Navigator,** Cadamosto's involvement in the exploration of the African coast was partially accidental. He had initially intended to sail to Flanders as part of the crew of the Venetian merchant galley with his brother.

19. This initial journey was delayed in Portugal because of unfavorable weather, during which time **Cadamosto was approached by Prince Henry's** representatives, who offered him the possibility of setting sail to the western coast of Africa to explore it.

20. **Cadamosto agreed, believing that it was his destiny to undertake such an ambitious endeavor,** and left his crewmates to prepare for the sponsored expedition.

21. In March of 1455, **Cadamosto set sail with a Portuguese caravel along the West African coast,** with the expedition thoroughly examining whatever they encountered along the way.

22. Ultimately, the expedition would result in **Cadamosto and his men mapping most of the western African coastline,** taking note of the local peoples and geographic features of the unknown land.

23. The **expedition discovered the mouth of the Gambian River in the summer of 1455,** where they experienced resistance from local people who pelted them with missiles.

24. **Cadamosto and his crew tried to limit direct contact with the African natives** as much as possible to avoid conflict and preserve manpower.

25. **They returned back to Portugal** by the end of the year, taking with them several African captives.

26. In 1456, **Cadamosto set out to explore the African coast again,** this time setting sail with a larger expedition to expand upon his previous journey.

27. **The second expedition was launched from the port city of Lagos** in May of 1456 and followed much of the same route as the first one.

28. Throughout his adventures, **Cadamosto kept a detailed diary in which he described each major development on the journeys.**

29. Thanks to the publication of this document, **Europeans' knowledge of Africa became much greater.**

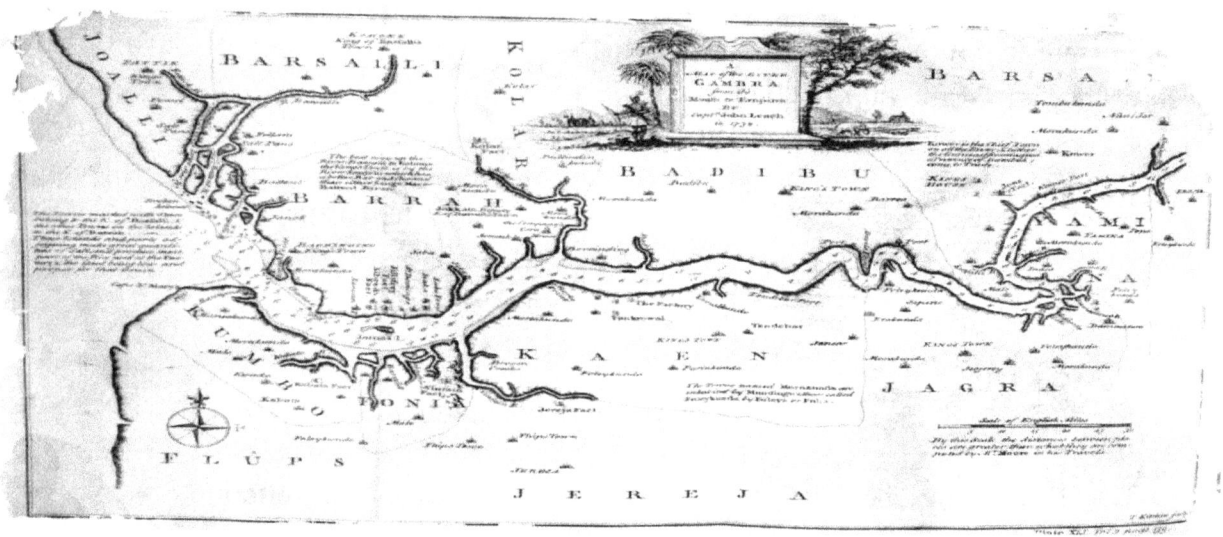

Christopher Columbus's Voyages to the Americas
(1492–1504)

This chapter will explore Christopher Columbus's voyages to the Americas. We'll discover fifteen interesting facts about his journey, including where he went and what he discovered. We'll learn how **these expeditions helped shape Europe's understanding of the world** and led to increased trade.

30. **Christopher Columbus was an Italian explorer** who made four trips to the Americas from 1492 to 1504.

31. Before setting sail, **Columbus aimed to secure funding from the Portuguese Crown.** He was denied, forcing him to go to Spain to ask for funds there instead.

32. In 1492, **Christopher Columbus sailed from Spain** in search of a westward sea route to India with a fleet of three ships.

33. **Columbus believed that he could reach India sailing to the west because of the circumference of the Earth.** He underestimated the Earth's circumference, though, believing the world was much smaller than it actually is.

34. **He arrived in the Caribbean on October 12th and believed he had found the East Indies.** The indigenous people who lived there were referred to as Indians.

35. **Columbus and his men encountered the indigenous Taíno people.** Columbus sought to establish friendly relations with the Taíno, but as tensions escalated, he resorted to using violent methods to subjugate them.

36. On his first voyage, **Columbus explored Cuba, Hispaniola** (now Haiti and the Dominican Republic), **Jamaica, and other nearby islands.**

37. **On his second voyage to the Americas, he explored several Caribbean islands and set up a colony called La Isabela,** but it didn't work out because of unfriendly natives and bad weather.

38. **The second trip was much larger.** Seventeen vessels carried hundreds of voyagers who sought to settle new lands in the Indies.

39. **Many of them were farmers or laborers.** They came to acquire land of their own so they could become wealthy and influential.

40. During this journey, **Columbus discovered Trinidad and Tobago,** located off the coast of Venezuela.

41. **He explored Central America on his fourth voyage** (1502–1504).

42. In 1503, **he set sail for Hispaniola once again but was forced into Jamaica due to bad weather.** He was stranded there until 1504.

43. **Columbus established Spanish colonies throughout the Caribbean and Central America,** but most of them failed.

44. **Spanish colonies grew exponentially in the New World,** allowing Spain to become one of the wealthiest empires in Europe.

Portuguese Exploration of India
(1497–1641)

The Portuguese exploration of India was a pivotal time in the history of Europe's interactions with Asia. In this chapter, we will explore eighteen fascinating facts about Portuguese voyages to India and the subsequent colonization that took place there.

45. In 1497, **the Portuguese explorer named Vasco da Gama sailed from Portugal to India.**

46. **He arrived in Calicut** (now called Kozhikode), a port city on the southwest coast, and was welcomed by local rulers.

47. **The zamorin (king) of Calicut gave da Gama permission to trade and establish trading posts.**

48. **Upon da Gama's return to Portugal in September 1499,** he brought valuable gifts such as spices and silks from India, which had been considered luxurious commodities in Europe since ancient times.

49. **King Manuel I of Portugal ordered more ships be sent to further explore** and create trade opportunities with Asian countries, including China and the Java Islands.

50. **While the Portuguese were initially well received by local rulers like those at Cochin** (Kochi) and **Cannanore** (Kannur), tensions began rising between them due to various factors like cultural differences.

51. **In order to better control its territories in India, Portugal established the Viceroyalty of Portuguese India in September 1505,** which would survive for the next four centuries.

52. **Francisco de Almeida became the first viceroy of Portuguese India,** managing to establish a strong naval presence in the region and contributing to Portugal's economic gains from the new viceroyalty.

53. In 1509, **Afonso de Albuquerque was appointed governor of Portuguese settlements in India** and arrived in Calicut with a fleet of ships to establish the first Portuguese trading post there.

54. **He then set his sights on conquering Goa,** an island off the **Indian coast that had been under Muslim rule** since 1469. He successfully captured it after a three-month siege in 1510.

55. **Goa became the capital of Portuguese India** and a major hub for trade and administration.

56. **This strategic victory opened many more trade routes for Portugal** and provided the Portuguese access to valuable resources such as spices and ivory from East Africa, such as the present-day countries of Mozambique and Somalia.

57. **The Portuguese built several impressive churches and forts throughout India.** One example was St. Paul's Church in Old Goa, which still stands today.

58. **The powerful presence of Portugal brought about a wave of Christianity in South Asia,** with missionary activities being undertaken from its center at Goa.

59. **The Goa Inquisition,** which was set up in 1561, introduced an array of oppressive measures and persecuted **many non-Christian religions of India, forcing thousands to convert.**

60. By the late 16th century, **Portugal had become one of the most influential powers in Asia,** with strongholds in India, China, and East Africa.

61. **Portugal would go on to enjoy almost total dominance in the Indian Ocean** before the arrival of the Dutch, who challenged the Portuguese claims in Malaysia and Indonesia in the 17th century.

62. **Portugal would leave behind an indelible mark on South Asian culture,** as seen through its architecture, cuisine, and language. These influences are still present today.

Portuguese Exploration of Brazil
(1500–1700)

In this chapter, **explore the incredible history of Portuguese exploration in Brazil** from 1500 to 1700. We will uncover sixteen interesting facts about colonization, trade networks, culture clashes, and more.

63. In 1500, **the Portuguese became the first European country to colonize Brazil.**

64. **The Brazilian coast was explored by a Portuguese explorer named Pedro Álvares Cabral** in April of that year.

65. **He named the area Terra de Vera Cruz, which means "Land of the True Cross,"** and claimed it for Portugal when he landed on its shores.

66. In 1501, **Italian explorer Amerigo Vespucci, who had previously been on a voyage with Christopher Columbus,** arrived in Brazil with the Portuguese and took part in the exploration of the area. His presence in Brazil is sometimes disputed.

67. **The whole continent would be named South America** after Amerigo Vespucci by a German cartographer named Martin Waldseemüller. **Vespucci was one of the first Europeans to realize that the land that had been discovered was not part of India.**

68. **Eventually, Portugal would come into contact with the native population of Brazil— the Tupi people**—who lived in small communities along the coast.

69. In 1500, **Portugal made Brazil a royal colony**, but it wasn't until 1549 that the Portuguese Crown established the Governorate General of Brazil, effectively establishing colonial administration.

70. **The name of the colony, Brazil, was derived from the local brazilwood tree,** which was considered a valuable commodity because of the distinct red dye that could be obtained from manufacturing it.

71. In 1565, **the Portuguese founded Rio de Janeiro in the southern part of Brazil,** a city that would ultimately serve as Brazil's capital from 1763 to 1960.

72. **Rio soon become an important trading port thanks to its strategic location** and navigable rivers connecting inland areas of Brazil with the rest of the continent.

73. By the mid-16th century, **Portuguese Jesuits had arrived in Brazil** and started building schools and churches while converting indigenous peoples to Catholicism.

74. By 1600, **most of today's modern cities like Salvador, the colony's first capital, and Recife had already been established.** European influences could be seen in their architecture and culture.

75. **When gold was discovered inland near Ouro Preto in Minas Gerais** during the late 17th century, hundreds of settlers flocked to the area, resulting in an increase in commercial activities within Brazilian territory.

76. **Slavery became increasingly common due to the need for labor in mines or plantations** and for those who could not afford to pay their taxes.

77. **Brazil soon assumed principal economic importance for Portugal.** For a long time, Brazil was the world's largest sugar and, later on, coffee producer.

78. **Brazil would be Portugal's largest colony by far.** It would become independent in the 19th century in 1822.

Piracy, Privateering, and the Atlantic Slave Trade
(1500–1722)

This chapter takes a closer look at the history of piracy, privateering, and the Atlantic slave trade. We'll discover fifteen fascinating facts about pirates and privateers, their motivations for attacking, and the impact of anti-piracy laws on international trade routes.

79. During the 16th and 17th centuries, **piracy became a major problem in the Atlantic Ocean.**

80. **Piracy was so widespread during this period** that it began to negatively affect international trade routes, primarily impacting Europe, Africa, and North America.

81. **In response to piratical activity, many countries passed anti-piracy laws,** such as England's Navigation Acts.

82. **The Navigation Acts prohibited foreign ships from trading with their colonies without paying taxes first.**

83. **Governments would recruit ships,** known as **privateers**, which were authorized to attack enemy or pirate ships.

84. **The most famous group of privateers was known as the Brethren of the Coast,** which operated mainly around Central America and the Caribbean Sea in the 17th century.

85. **The Atlantic slave trade was a large part of international trade during this period** and saw millions of Africans being sold as slaves across the world.

86. **Privateers were involved in the slave trade,** though not to the same extent as regular slave traders.

87. **Captain William Kidd was one of the most prominent privateers of his time;** originally from Scotland, he had made his name all over the Atlantic, often employed by the British Crown to protect British interests in North America.

88. **Many pirates formed their own "pirate republics,"** which were safe havens where they would be safe from government prosecution or interference as long as they respected local laws.

89. **The Barbary Corsairs were some of the fiercest pirates at sea in the 17th century.** They mainly preyed on European ships in the Mediterranean Sea.

90. In 1698, **Britain passed its first act against piracy,** which gave more power to naval forces at sea and allowed for harsher punishments for those caught pirating or privateering.

91. **Edward Teach, or "Blackbeard," was an infamous British pirate and the captain of Queen Anne's Revenge,** a pirate ship that terrorized shipping lanes around North America before it ran aground off of what is now North Carolina in 1718.

92. In 1713, **the Treaty of Utrecht was signed between Britain and France,** which included provisions about privateering related to these countries.

93. **Privateering was fully denounced and abolished as a practice in the 19th century** with the Declaration of Paris in 1856.

Juan Díaz de Solís's Discovery of the Rio de la Plata
(1515–1516)

In this chapter, we will explore Juan Díaz de Solís's discovery of the Rio de la Plata. Join us as we uncover seventeen interesting facts about his journey, from discovering native tribes to the territories he explored.

94. **Juan Díaz de Solís was a Spanish explorer who set out in 1515 to find the legendary city of El Dorado and its riches.**

95. **His voyage took him south along the Atlantic coast** of South America to what is now Argentina and Uruguay.

96. On his journey, **he discovered a large estuary river, which he named Rio de la Plata, meaning "Silver River" in Spanish,** due to reports that silver could be found within its banks.

97. In December 1515, **he encountered several indigenous tribes,** including **the Charrúa** (from present-day Uruguay) and **the Guarani** (from today's Paraguay).

98. **The estuary of the river was briefly explored by Fernando Magellan,** who reached the mouth of the river during his voyage in 1520 before continuing the journey to circumnavigate the world.

99. His exact cause of death is unknown, and it **is even believed that Díaz de Solís drowned in the Rio de la Plata.**

100. In 1516, **Álvar Nuñez Cabeza de Vaca took over the leadership of the expedition** and continued to explore the Rio de la Plata.

101. **Despite the hostile environment and a lack of resources, Díaz de Solís's expedition was successful** in mapping out much of what is now known as Argentina and Uruguay.

102. **From this discovery, a new trade route opened up between Spain and South America,** enabling merchants to directly access goods such as silver.

103. **The Rio de la Plata would prove to be an important gateway for colonists** looking to settle in South America. It was an entry point into the continent.

104. **Settlers would go on to form Buenos Aires,** which became one of the largest cities in South America, near the mouth of the river.

105. Over time, **more discoveries were made in the region,** including the discovery of several indigenous peoples who had not been contacted before, such as **the Chaná and Yaro tribes.**

106. **After the exploration of South America, Spain and Portugal divided the new colonies** according to the demarcation line made in 1494 in the Treaty of Tordesillas.

107. According to the treaty, **all of the lands colonized and explored would be divided by the two nations** on either sides of the meridian 370 leagues west of Cape Verde.

108. **Díaz de Solís's discovery brought fame for himself,** as well as great wealth to Spain.

109. **The Rio de la Plata is now known as one of the largest estuaries in the world,** measuring around four hundred kilometers long and sixty-four kilometers wide.

110. **The prosperity of the region** and the many advantages it was associated with resulted in several conflicts that were concentrated around the area; **Brazil, Uruguay, Argentina, and Paraguay challenged each other for control** during the 19th century.

Hernán Cortés and the Spanish Conquest of Mexico and Central America (1518–1521)

This chapter will explore the history of Spanish settlement in Mexico and Central America. We'll take a look at over thirty interesting facts about the Spaniards' journey, the cities they founded, their interactions with the natives, and how the conquest affected the region.

111. In 1518, **a Spanish army led by Pedro de Alvarado** and other explorers set sail from Spain to explore the area now known as Central America.

112. **The first stop during their journey was Cuba,** where they met up with **Hernán Cortés,** a lesser Spanish noble who had journeyed to the New World for a new life.

113. **Cortés became the captain of the expedition.** He went on to explore the mainland, reaching Mexico and founding the city of Veracruz in August 1519.

114. **The expedition encountered the Aztecs and Maya,** giving them the chance to learn about different cultures and customs in Mexico and Central America.

115. **The Aztecs were an advanced civilization living in what are now parts of Mexico, Guatemala, and Belize.**

116. **Their capital was the great city of Tenochtitlan on Lake Texcoco.** There were more than 200,000 inhabitants at the time of the arrival of the conquistadors.

117. **The Aztecs were fierce warriors.** They had subjugated their neighboring tribes and emerged as their suzerains, taking tribute from the smaller tribes.

118. **Suspecting that the Aztecs had a lot of valuables, like gold, to plunder and eager to claim the unexplored territories for the Spanish Crown,** Cortés launched an invasion against the Aztecs upon his arrival in Mexico.

119. **Before the breakout of hostilities, Cortés and his crew were initially received in a friendly manner by Aztec Emperor Montezuma II in Tenochtitlan.** The Spaniards were amazed by how advanced the city was.

120. **The Spanish would be forced out of the city,** as tensions between the locals and the armed conquistadors resulted in a full-on conflict.

121. **Cortés returned after a couple of months to take the city.** He had about five hundred soldiers at his disposal, but he was soon joined by hundreds of locals along the way. They wanted him to overthrow the Aztec oppressors.

122. **The Spanish had guns. Most of the natives used only spears, bows and arrows,** or swords made from stone or wood. This gave the Spanish a huge advantage.

123. **The Spaniards used horses during combat,** which terrified some tribes since they had never seen them before.

124. **Cortés's leadership, the help of local native tribes,** European weaponry, and the spread of disease helped topple the Aztec Empire.

125. **After conquering the Aztec Empire, Cortés became governor of New Spain** (present-day Mexico).

126. **On the ruins of the plundered Aztec capital, the Spanish built their own city, Mexico City,** which would become the center of operations in New Spain.

127. After conquering much of central Mexico over the next few years, **Spanish possessions would be reorganized into a new imperial viceroyalty called the Viceroyalty of New Spain.**

128. **The viceroyalty would grow over time** to include Mexico, Central America, parts of the Caribbean, and parts of the United States.

129. **Spanish colonists organized their lands into encomiendas,** possessions where they were royally permitted to employ the indigenous populations for agricultural labor.

130. **The Spanish also brought many deadly diseases with them.** The native populations had not previously been exposed to these diseases, which means their immune systems did not know how to respond to them.

131. **Millions of natives throughout Mexico, the Caribbean, Central America, South America, and North America died due to diseases.**

132. **One of the reasons Cortés was able to take Tenochtitlan** was because of a smallpox epidemic that had broken out in the city during the Spaniards' first visit there.

133. **The Aztecs were able to drive out the Spanish from Tenochtitlan on one occasion,** briefly regaining control of the city; however, they were eventually too weakened to put up more resistance to the conquistadors.

134. **The conquistadors took over Tenochtitlan and developed it according to their needs;** the city became a center for Spanish operations in North America in 1521.

135. **The Americas also had many novelties for the Spaniards, such as tobacco.**

136. **The Spanish conquest marked an important shift** from traditional indigenous cultures toward a more European way of life.

137. **The introduction of Christianity would become an important part of the Spaniards' mission.** They sought to convert locals living in New Spain to Catholicism. They obtained permission from the papacy to do so.

138. **The Spaniards introduced new agricultural practices** that greatly boosted the production capabilities of native economies; they also diversified the output by bringing new crops like wheat into the Americas.

139. **During this era, many conquistadors searched for gold and silver throughout New Spain.** In fact, valuable minerals were some of the main reasons behind colonization.

140. By the end of the 16th century, **Mexico City, alongside Veracruz and Guadalajara, had become a major center in New Spain,** facilitating trade and movement of Spaniards throughout the colony.

141. **With the development of cities came new social classes. Spanish-born Spaniards** were at the top of the hierarchy. They owned most of the land, which they had conquered from the natives.

142. **Native people who converted to Christianity, mixed-race individuals** (known as mestizos), and even Spaniards who had been born in the colonies were below the Spaniards in society.

143. **Cortés's conquests encouraged other Spanish explorers to explore other parts of America** in hopes of finding new riches or land.

144. His success, coupled with other explorations during the 16th century, eventually resulted in an estimated number of up to 2 million **Spaniards moving from Europe to the Americas during the era of Spanish colonization** until the 19th century.

The Establishment of the Viceroyalty of New Spain
(1535– 1542)

This chapter will explore the establishment of the Viceroyalty of New Spain. We'll take a look at sixteen interesting facts about its formation, figures, and more.

145. In 1535, **King Charles V of Spain created the Viceroyalty of New Spain** to help him rule what is now Mexico and Central America.

146. **The first viceroy was Antonio de Mendoza, who arrived in New Spain** in 1535 and served until 1550, after which he also briefly served as the Spanish Viceroy of Peru.

147. **The new colony would eventually cover a huge area** that stretched from modern-day Louisiana to Central America, including much of present-day Mexico and Peru, as well as some Caribbean islands like Cuba and Puerto Rico.

148. **The official language was Spanish, but many local languages were also spoken by the native people there, such as Nahuatl** (the Aztec language) or Mayan.

149. **To make sure everyone followed Spanish laws,** a court system called **audiencias** was set up in each city. Judges heard cases related to civil disputes or criminal accusations against officials or citizens.

150. **The Viceroyalty of New Spain was divided into different administrative districts known as intendencies.** They would gradually grow in number as the viceroyalty expanded its borders.

151. In the mid-16th century, **a port called San Juan de Ulúa was built along the Gulf of Mexico** to protect the newly formed colony from enemy attacks or foreign intrusions.

lo en la yglesia Paroquial de S. Bertolome o Solo tepec, el dia
delo Proxulo por el S. Juin vgini . . . tregoria juisu
Grador Onkrievico . . . Sagra . . .

152. **To promote trade with Europe, a system of galleons was created that transported goods** between Veracruz and Cádiz, Spain, for many years.

153. **The Viceroyalty of New Spain would experience population decline** largely due to the spread of deadly diseases from Europeans to the native populations, but the situation stabilized by the 1600s.

154. **African slaves were brought over by Spanish merchants,** who traded them along with other merchandise to local rulers throughout Central and South America.

155. **To keep everyone safe from disease, all ships arriving in the port of Veracruz were quarantined for two weeks** before they could enter the city.

156. **Over time, Veracruz emerged as one of the largest port cities of the Viceroyalty of New Spain.** The city retained its importance even after decolonization and the independence of Mexico.

157. **To make sure that New Spain remained loyal to its king, Charles V sent many of his trusted officials** to monitor the colony's governance.

158. By the 1600s, **several religious orders had been established throughout New Spain,** including the Franciscan, Dominican, and Augustinian orders. Their main goal was to convert native people to Christianity through missionary work.

159. **Viceroy Luis de Velasco, the second viceroy of the colony, was a very influential leader** who expanded New Spain's economic activities. He was somewhat popular among the natives because he helped defend them.

160. **The Viceroyalty of New Spain remained active until 1821** when it was replaced by the independent Republic of Mexico after a successful war of independence against the Spanish Empire.

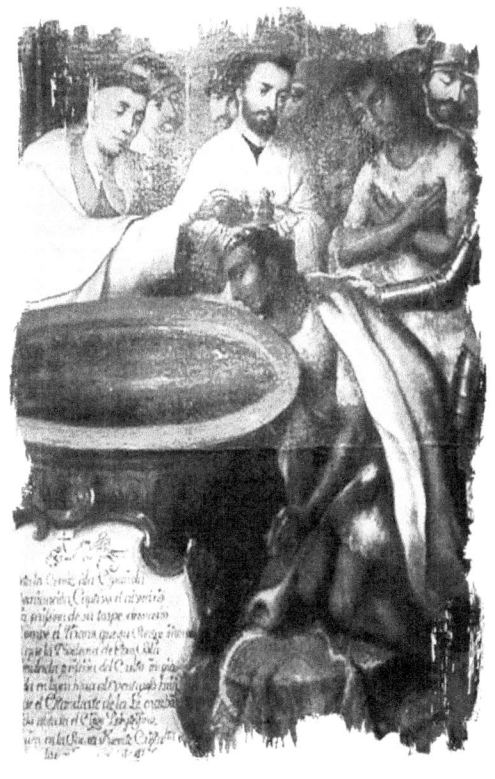

Spanish Conquests of Central and South America

(1521–1571)

This chapter will explore the often-overlooked history of Spanish conquests in Central and South America. We'll delve into over thirty facts about how these conquests were carried out, **including details on the weaponry and tactics** used and the effects of the conquest both during and after this period.

161. **Conquistadors arrived in other parts of Central America** around the same time as Cortés was conquering the Aztecs.

162. **Many Central and South American indigenous peoples died due to the European diseases,** such as smallpox and influenza, brought by the Spaniards.

163. At that time, **the Yucatán Peninsula was inhabited mostly by the Maya,** who had a rather advanced culture with an interesting pantheon of gods.

164. **Although the Maya had already been weakened by the time of the Spaniards' arrival,** they held out against the Spanish until 1697, over 150 years after the Spanish first arrived.

165. In 1513, **General Vasco Núñez de Balboa's expedition crossed the Panama Isthmus between the Atlantic and Pacific Oceans.** The conquistadors would consolidate their control over Panama afterward.

166. **Pedro de Alvarado is the man credited for the Spanish conquest of what is now Guatemala in 1524.**

167. In 1525, **the conquest of Honduras began. Francisco de Montejo, the leader of the expedition,** was appointed as its first Spanish governor.

168. **Some of these expeditions were organized to find the mystical El Dorado,** a city established by an indigenous tribe that was allegedly built of gold.

169. **Spain started to cement its control of Nicaragua** in the 1520s.

170. By the late 1570s, **some parts of Central America had been pacified,** although there were plenty of rebellions by indigenous populations.

171. **Spanish conquistador Francisco Pizarro led an expedition in western South America** from 1526 to 1542.

172. **He discovered the Inca Empire**, one of the most powerful native empires in the Americas. It was centered in Peru and Chile.

173. **The Inca civilization had many settlements in the mountains.** The civilization centered around the city of Cuzco in Peru.

174. They spoke the Quechua language but did not have a formal writing system.

175. **The Incas did not use the wheel for transportation purposes.** They did not have steel or iron, but they did use bronze and copper for their tools and weapons.

176. **Francisco Pizarro launched several different expeditions** from Central America south into the Inca territories.

177. **He eventually defeated and captured the Inca leader, Atahualpa**, in 1532.

178. **The conquistadors pillaged the Inca lands,** taking large amounts of gold and silver from sacred temples and cities.

179. **In April 1533, Atahualpa was put on trial for treason.** He agreed to convert to die by strangulation instead of being burned alive.

180. **Atahualpa had agreed to pay a ransom of gold in exchange for his release.** He provided the Spanish with a room full of silver.

181. **After the capture and execution of their leader, many Incas revolted against Pizarro's rule,** which led to several battles.

182. **In 1536, the Incas finally surrendered due to a lack of resources and manpower.**

183. **Pizarro founded the city of Lima** in 1535, near where he had conquered Cajamarca.

184. By late 1538, nearly **all Inca territories were under Spanish control.** The conquistadors would consolidate their control over time.

185. Over the next few years, **Pizarro continued expanding Spain's reach into Peru with military force.** Christianity and European customs were also introduced to the native people.

186. **Pizarro was awarded the titles of governor and captain-general by King Charles V** for his successful mission.

187. **Many expeditions were launched in South America after Pizarro defeated the Incas.**

188. **The Viceroyalty of Peru was the second most important overseas territory of Spain** during the era of colonization until its formal dissolution in 1824; it was succeeded by the newly independent South American nations.

189. **The conquest of Bolivia by the Spanish began in 1532, with Diego de Almagro,** a former crewmate of Pizarro, leading an expedition there.

190. **Francisco de Orellana, another participant in Pizarro's conquest,** later led an exploration of the Amazon River to its mouth at the Atlantic Ocean in Portuguese Brazil in the 1540s.

191. **La Paz was founded in 1548 by Alonso de Mendoza.** It became the official capital of Spanish Bolivia.

192. **An interesting figure in the Spanish colonization of South America is actually a German man named Ambrosius Ehinger** (Ambrosio Alfinger in Spanish). He explored parts of

northeastern South America, founding the city of Maracaibo in 1529.

193. **Ehinger was sent to colonize South America by the wealthy Welser family,** who had been granted concessions by **King Charles V of Spain** (who was also the emperor of the Holy Roman Empire). Their charter would be revoked in the 1540s.

194. Spanish **expeditions established settlements all along Colombia's Caribbean coastlines until the Orinoco River Basin in Venezuela.**

Magellan's Circumnavigation of the Globe (1519–1522)

This chapter will explore the incredible feat of navigation accomplished by **Ferdinand Magellan** and his crew in 1522. We'll take a look at over thirty interesting facts about their journey, from why they embarked on it to how many ships survived the circumnavigation.

195. **Ferdinand Magellan led a fleet of five ships and about 270 sailors on an expedition** to sail around the world in 1519.

196. **Just like Columbus, he wanted to find a way from Europe to Asia by sailing west instead of east,** which was how people usually traveled during that time.

197. **The journey lasted three years,** ending on September 6th, 1522.

198. **Only one ship, the Victoria, managed to return home after completing the mission.**

199. **The initial goal of Magellan's expedition was to reach the fabled Spice Islands,** about whose location the Europeans knew very little.

200. **The islands were called Spice Islands because they had lots of spices like cinnamon, clove, and nutmeg growing there.** These spices were all valuable and would sell for high prices in European markets.

201. **The Spice Islands refer to the modern-day Maluku Islands** in the eastern part of the Indonesian archipelago.

202. **The route the expedition chose would first reach South America.** Then, the men would sail southward along its eastern coast, hoping they could somehow get around the continent and make it to East Asia.

203. **Magellan and his crew managed to successfully sail around South America,** making stops along the way, including at the recently founded Portuguese ports in Brazil.

204. **They crossed a very narrow strait in the south of the continent to reach the Pacific Ocean.** Today, that strait is called the Magellan Strait.

205. **Magellan would name the Pacific Ocean**, which had previously been unexplored by the colonizers. **He called it "Pacific" because it looked so peaceful compared to other seas** he had encountered.

206. **While traversing the biggest ocean on the Earth, Magellan made a couple of stops** on small Pacific islands before finally reaching the Indonesian archipelago.

207. **Navigating through the Indonesian islands proved to be very difficult.** The waters were completely unexplored by the Europeans, and the natives were, at times, very hostile to them.

208. **After escaping danger in Bali, Magellan arrived at Ternate Island,** where he met **the sultan of Tidore,** who welcomed him warmly with gifts of spices and supplies.

209. **Magellan stayed in the Spice Islands for two months,** trading goods with the locals and exploring other nearby islands like Ambon and Timor.

210. While in the area, **Magellan mapped out much of Indonesia's coastline,** which would be used by future explorers who followed his journey.

211. **Magellan died during the expedition on Mactan Island** in April 1521 during a conflict with the natives.

212. **Most of the ships had been damaged or destroyed by that time,** so they were abandoned.

213. **One of Magellan's captains completed the circumnavigation on his behalf nine months later,** with seventeen other members of the crew reaching Europe in 1522.

214. **Magellan's expedition was the first one to go around the world by sea,** proving the theory that the Earth was round.

215. **It showed the proficiency of contemporary ships,** which could sail for long distances without needing to stop for constant maintenance along the way.

216. **Magellan's crew encountered many different cultures and languages,** making their voyage a journey of discovery for both them and the Europeans at home.

217. **In addition to proving the circumference of the Earth,** the journey opened up new trade routes between Europe and Asia.

218. **These routes allowed goods from these two regions to be exchanged** with each other faster than ever before.

219. **Magellan's expedition also motivated many European nations to try their hand at exploration,** helping launch a new wave of colonization in the Americas and Southeast Asia.

220. **The route taken by Magellan's fleet has been followed by numerous explorers, including Captain Cook** in the mid-18th century, who mapped out much of Australia during his voyage.

221. **Though Magellan was Portuguese, he embarked on a Spanish expedition.** He was accompanied by a Spanish navigator.

222. **However, Portugal would end up exploiting Magellan's travels.** Having a natural maritime advantage over the other European states, Portugal would be the first nation to actively start the colonization of Southeast Asia.

223. **During this time, Portuguese colonizers and traders formed alliances with local leaders** to gain control over spice production on the islands.

224. **This allowed them access to valuable resources like pepper, nutmeg, and cloves** that could only be found there.

225. **The Portuguese exploration of the Spice Islands opened up new trade routes,** which led to an age of globalization that changed world history forever.

Jacques Cartier's Exploration of the Saint Lawrence River (1534)

This chapter explores the groundbreaking explorations of French explorer Jacques Cartier. We'll discover several interesting facts about his journey to the Saint Lawrence River and how it changed history.

226. **Jacques Cartier was a French explorer** who sailed to the Saint Lawrence River in 1534.

227. **He was commissioned by King Francis I of France** to find a passage from the Atlantic Ocean to Asia through North America.

228. **Cartier explored what is now known as Canada.** On July 24th, 1534, he arrived at Stadacona (now Quebec City).

229. **Cartier was the first European to explore and map out the Saint Lawrence River Basin.**

230. **During his journey, he made contact with local Native American tribes** and learned about their culture and language, which included words like "canoe" and "toboggan."

231. **He named the newly discovered land Canada,** a name that stemmed from the native Iroquoian word for settlement (Kanata).

232. Supposedly, **Cartier heard the name uttered by the locals** when they directed him toward a neighboring settlement in the area of modern-day Quebec.

233. **In September of that year, Cartier traveled farther upriver toward Hochelaga** (Montreal), where he encountered a village inhabited by the local Iroquois people.

234. **The crew was able to map out rivers, such as the Saguenay River, for future expeditions.**

235. **In 1535, Cartier returned to France with two young Native American men he had taken as guides and interpreters.** The king allowed Cartier to bring them back.

236. **Cartier was also accompanied by a cargo of valuable goods, such as furs and beaver pelts,** which were highly sought after in Europe at this time.

237. On his second trip, which lasted from 1535 to 1536, **Jacques Cartier explored farther upriver toward Montreal,** but due to hostile encounters with local Iroquoians, they were forced to turn back before reaching their destination.

238. **Through these explorations, he charted much of what we know today about the Saint Lawrence River,** including islands like Anticosti.

239. Interestingly, much like Columbus, **Jacques Cartier was at first sure that he had reached the Asian continent** instead of having discovered an entirely new landmass.

240. **His voyages helped establish trading relationships between France and Canada** for the fur trade, which lasted over two hundred years.

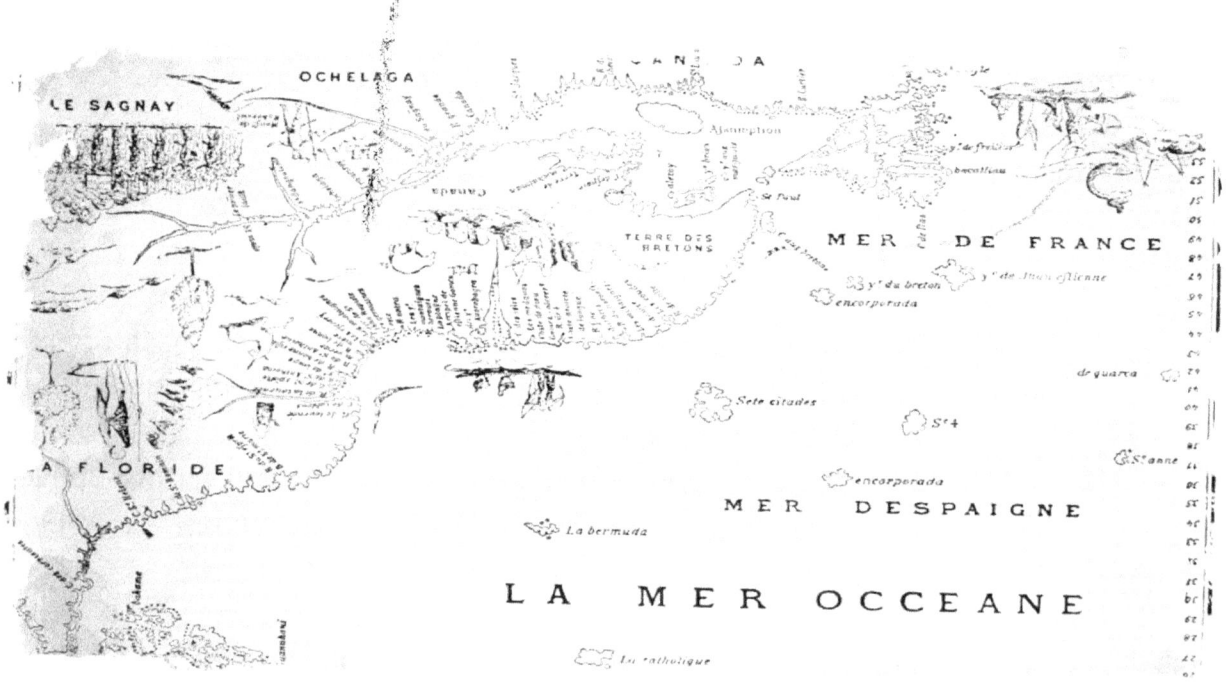

Cartography and Technology in the Age of Discovery

The Age of Discovery went hand in hand with many contemporary technological advancements that stimulated the efforts to explore the world and get to know it better. This chapter will cover some of the most important developments that took place during this period.

241. **The era of innovation brought about in Europe that resulted in the Age of Discovery** was complemented by a previously unseen level of technological advancements in all fields of life.

242. **These advancements were used by explorers and affected the way they perceived the world around them.** New tools also helped them navigate their way through the oceans.

243. **One of the most important developments was cartography,** the method of scientifically creating maps.

244. **The revival of cartography was caused by the rediscovery of ancient maps** and sources in the Renaissance that had been lost during the Middle Ages.

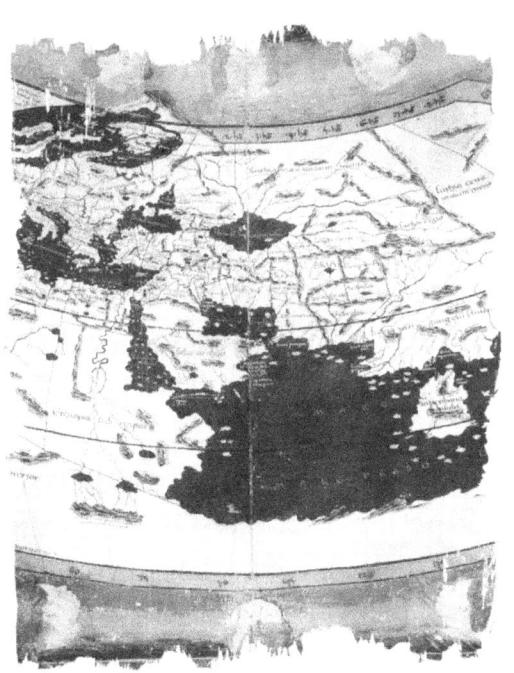

245. **As Europeans began to discover the New World, they increasingly needed to advance their map-making systems.** Many voyages, like Magellan's circumnavigation of the world, helped build the basic skeleton of a world map that was then expanded upon again and again.

246. **The caravel was a new type of ship, smaller and highly maneuverable,** which was crucial for long sea voyages. It allowed European sailors to explore further and faster than before.

247. **Although Italian scientist Galileo Galilei is not considered to be the inventor of the telescope, he did improve it,** allowing him and other people around the world to see celestial objects much more clearly.

248. **Many explorers used modified telescopes to scout the seas and observe the heavens.**

249. **The magnetic compass, which had been developed by the Chinese, became a vital tool for European navigators during the Age of Discovery.** It allowed sailors to determine direction even during cloudy or foggy conditions when stars were not visible.

250. **The astrolabe, an instrument used to observe the position of the stars and planets,** was adapted from earlier Middle Eastern designs. It became essential for celestial navigation, helping to determine latitude.

251. **The quadrant and sextant, which followed the astrolabe,** allowed for more precise measurements of latitude and, eventually, longitude.

252. **The French philosopher René Descartes** introduced what is now known as **Cartesian coordinate geometry** in 1637. This advancement revolutionized mathematics by linking algebraic equations to geometric shapes for visualization purposes.

253. **Coordinate geometry made it possible to better put down the discoveries of the explorers on the map** and to create a unified, objective system of perceiving things in two dimensions.

254. **Carolus Linnaeus developed a new, easier, and systematic way to classify living things,** which he published in his work Systema Naturae in 1735.

255. **This introduced ways to gather information about new wildlife** Europeans encountered on other continents, providing a foundation for the development of later disciplines.

256. **Introduced by Johannes Gutenberg in the mid-15th century, the printing press** enabled the mass production of maps and nautical charts, which were previously hand-drawn and rare. This spread geographic knowledge more widely and rapidly.

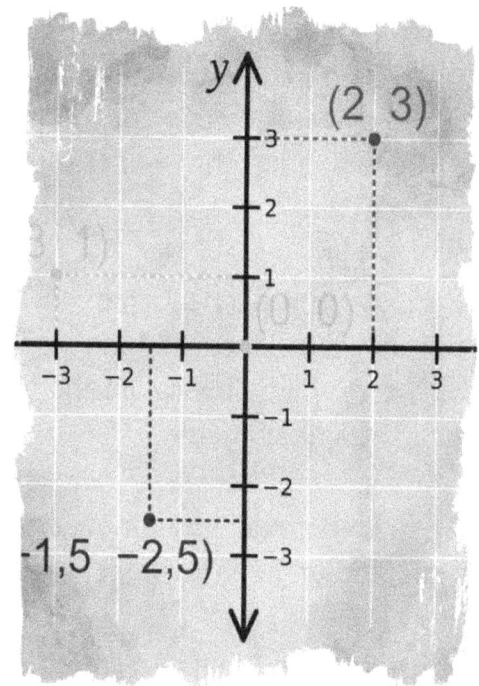

Jesuits in the Americas
(1549–1830)

This chapter will explore the fascinating history of Jesuit missionaries in the Americas. We'll delve into interesting facts about their mission to spread Catholicism among indigenous people, how they interacted with different cultures, and the lasting legacy of this period.

257. **In 1549, the first Jesuits arrived in South America to spread Catholicism** among the indigenous people who lived there.

258. During the late 16th century, **Jesuit missionaries began traveling to Central America and Mexico** to convert local tribes and build churches and schools.

259. By 1600, **a significant number of Jesuits were working in Latin America as teachers,** preachers, or healers of spiritual or physical illnesses.

260. **We know of their travels and activities through their own accounts.** One of the most famous accounts came from Dominican friar **Bartolomé de las Casas,** A Short Account of the Destruction of the Indies.

261. Between 1610 and 1650, **many Jesuit missions were established throughout Central and South America.**

262. **Nearly twenty million native people had converted by 1767.**

263. In the mid-1700s, **the central Spanish government started taking back control over its former colonies,** which meant that a lot of religious orders, like the Jesuits, faced expulsion.

264. In 1767, **the Spanish Crown ordered all Jesuits to be expelled from countries under Spanish rule.** Their missions were shut down.

265. **As a result of this expulsion, many thousands of native people lost access to education and spiritual guidance,** which had been provided by the Jesuit missionaries for many years.

266. **After being expelled from South America in 1767, some Jesuits moved northward into North America,** where they continued with their missionary work with Native American populations and other immigrants.

267. Since gaining independence, **the United States was one of the places that allowed the Jesuits complete freedom in their religious activities.**

268. During the 1700s, **Jesuits were actively involved in social justice movements** such as anti-slavery campaigns.

269. **Through their work with Native Americans and other immigrant communities, the Jesuits built up strong relationships,** which enabled them to gain access to regions that had previously been difficult for Europeans to penetrate.

270. **The legacy left behind by these early Jesuit missionaries is still visible today through educational institutions like Georgetown University or monuments** to honor indigenous people's culture.

Spanish Colonization of the Philippines (1565–1571)

The Spanish colonization of the Philippines is a fascinating period in history. This chapter will explore fifteen interesting facts about this era, from Spain's original failed attempt to their long rule of the islands.

271. **Spain first tried to colonize the Philippines in 1521 during Magellan's expedition but failed** because of bad weather, insufficient resources, and hostilities with the natives.

272. In 1565, another group of Spanish explorers, led by **Miguel López de Legazpi, arrived in the Philippines.**

273. **He established a settlement on the island of Cebu called San Miguel,** which was later moved to Manila Bay and renamed Intramuros ("within walls").

274. **The Spanish built forts around Intramuros** to protect against invaders such as Dutch or Chinese forces.

275. **Legazpi encountered local tribes,** some of whom were friendly and others who were hostile.

276. **Many Filipinos converted from traditional belief systems like animism to Christianity** during this period, sometimes even under threat of death if they did not comply with forced conversion efforts by Catholic clergymen accompanying the expedition.

277. **The Spanish brought the Latin alphabet and culture to the Philippines.**

278. **The Manila-Acapulco galleon trade route was established in 1565** and connected Mexico and the Philippines for over two hundred years.

279. **The Philippines was named after King Philip II of Spain.**

280. **One of the main goals of Spanish rule was to promote Christianity across Southeast Asia** and reduce the influence of other nations in neighboring lands.

281. **The Spanish created schools and churches dedicated to spreading Catholicism** and European ideals throughout the Philippines.

282. **Indigenous Filipinos acted mainly as tenant farmers or sharecroppers on lands** owned by wealthy families, including those with Spanish heritage.

283. **Spanish rule in the Philippines lasted for over three hundred years,** from 1565 to 1898.

284. **Some remnants of Spanish colonization still exist today,** such as many Filipino last names, language, architecture, religion, food, and customs.

285. **The Spanish colonization of the Philippines is historically significant.** It was a major contributor to cross-cultural exchange between Europe, Asia, and Latin America during this period.

English Voyages and Colonization of North America
(1585–1776)

This section will delve into the history of English colonization in North America, which began in the late 16th century. These North American colonies were the first to break free from their homeland, so we will also take a look at how these colonies achieved independence.

286. In the late 16th century, **English explorers set off on their first overseas exploration to colonize North America.**

287. **Sir Walter Raleigh led two voyages in 1584 and 1585 to explore the area** around present-day Roanoke Island, North Carolina.

288. In 1587, **John White was appointed governor of Roanoke Island** and sailed back to England for supplies.

289. **His ship was delayed to a war between Spain and England,** meaning that much-needed supplies couldn't make it back to the colonists.

290. **John White tried to send help from Britain multiple times.** In 1593, he went himself and found Roanoke empty with no clues besides the word "Croatoan" as to what happened to the colonists who disappeared.

291. **The mysterious disappearance of the Roanoke colonists has become a famous mystery.** The colony is sometimes referred to as the **"Lost Colony."**

292. **In 1607 another expedition from England arrived with more settlers who established their colony near the Chesapeake Bay.** This colony was known as Jamestown.

293. Founded in May, **it became Britain's first successful permanent settlement in the New World.**

294. **Jamestown served as the center of British operations in colonial North America** for the next few decades before the colonial enterprise grew to include much of the East Coast.

295. **The Jamestown colony became a royal charter company with the ability to create its own government and trade with local tribes** for fur and natural resources, setting the stage for British colonization in North America.

296. **The English initially sought gold and silver to become wealthy,** but the colonists eventually grew tobacco, which made some planters very wealthy.

297. **Native Americans had been living on the land for thousands of years before Europeans arrived.** Just like in Mexico, thousands were killed due to disease or conflicts with settlers.

298. Throughout the 17th century, more people traveled from **Britain** to North America, founding more towns where they could practice their own religious beliefs in peace.

299. **During this period, the English established trading posts in North America,** from Hudson Bay (Canada) to the Carolinas, along with several Caribbean islands.

300. By the 1620s, **English settlement was confined to the Eastern coast of the continent,** while **French settlers explored southward into Louisiana,** beginning an age of competition and warfare between rival European powers that shaped much of early American history.

301. **The Massachusetts Bay Colony was established in 1628,** with up to twenty thousand people migrating to areas around **Boston and Salem** throughout the next few years.

302. **Characterized by a large presence of Christian Puritans** who paved the way for its development, Massachusetts soon emerged as an important economic province for England in North America.

303. During this time, many other colonies were also formed, including **Maryland in 1632 and Rhode Island and Connecticut in 1633.**

304. From 1675 to 1676, **King Philip's War was waged.** It was fought between Native American tribes led by **Chief Metacom,** known as **"King Philip,"** and English colonists in New England.

305. **This ended with a victory for the colonial forces,** but it caused devastating losses to both sides, particularly the Native Americans, whose numbers had been significantly reduced due to European diseases.

306. **The Salem witch trials began in 1692 and became one of the most infamous events of this period.** More than two hundred people were accused of being witches, resulting in twenty executions.

307. In 1754, **a war between the French and the British called the Seven Years' War broke out in Europe,** which engulfed the two nations in a bloody struggle at every point of their contention around the world.

308. Interestingly, **much of the fighting was concentrated between the French and British colonists in North America,** where the British were joined by a confederation of Native American tribes.

309. **The British-Native American campaigns in 1759 were especially effective,** as they significantly weakened French positions in North America.

310. In 1763, **Pontiac's Rebellion broke out.** This rebellion was an unsuccessful attempt led by Ottawa Chief Pontiac to fight against British rule.

311. Ultimately, **Britain emerged victorious from the Seven Years' War in February of 1763,** leading to its hegemony over the colonial affairs of North America at the cost of about 160,000 lives.

312. **The British were able to negotiate a very favorable peace agreement,** which included ceding of French colonial possessions in North America on top of a substantial war reparation package that had to be paid by France.

313. **The Seven Years' War was an immensely influential conflict that affected the developments in Europe and the Americas** throughout the next few decades.

314. **It plunged both Great Britain and France into deep financial troubles,** as the nations had overspent throughout the duration of the war, leading them to increase taxes in their dependencies around the world.

315. **The Proclamation of 1763 was issued to protect Native American lands and prevent any further expansion into their territories by colonists.** This sparked a great deal of discontent among many settlers.

316. **The Stamp Act of 1765 made colonists pay taxes on all printed materials with an embossed stamp,** including newspapers, pamphlets, and legal documents.

317. On the evening of March 5th, 1770, **a confrontation between British soldiers and American colonists in Boston escalated into violence,** resulting in the deaths of five colonists.

318. **The discontent among the British colonies began to take shape into a real anti-British movement,** culminating in the events of December 16th, 1773, with the Boston Tea Party.

319. **Dozens of people disguised as Mohawk Indians dumped over three hundred chests of tea into Boston Harbor in 1773** to protest taxes that the colonists had no say in.

320. **The Boston Tea Party fueled resistance movements against the strict rule imposed by the British,** leading to **the American Revolutionary War**, which began in 1775.

321. **The colonists would secure their independence, breaking free from British rule and proclaiming the United States of America** in 1776, though the war itself would come to an end in 1783.

Dutch Exploration and Colonization of the Dutch East Indies
(1595–1945)

The Dutch exploration of the Dutch East Indies, the territory mostly comprising modern-day Indonesia, began in the late 16th century and led to the establishment of a colonial system that lasted until the mid-20th century. This section will dive deep into fascinating facts about Dutch voyages to the East Indies.

322. **The first Dutch expedition to the East Indies set sail in 1595.**

323. **The Dutch searched for a new trade route to Southeast Asia** that would bypass the established routes around Africa or through the Indian Ocean.

324. **The expedition was led by Cornelis de Houtman,** who first arrived in Java.

325. **De Houtman negotiated with the local rulers.** His efforts laid the groundwork for future trading rights and Dutch influence in the region.

326. Over time, **the natives traded spices and other local products for European goods,** mainly weapons.

327. **This expedition opened up new markets to Europeans.** Coffee and spices like pepper were especially popular.

328. **Many of these trading posts still exist today, as cities like Jakarta, Semarang, and Surabaya** were all expanded by the Dutch during their exploration period.

329. **The Netherlands continued to control much of Southeast Asia** until World War II, when Japan invaded Indonesia in the 1940s.

330. **Several fleets set sail from Europe headed toward what is now known as Indonesian waters between 1595 and 1605.** These ships brought back valuable goods, increasing the wealth of the Dutch.

331. Despite being relatively late to the colonial race, **the Dutch managed to quickly establish a hegemony on some of the most valuable products that flowed in from Southeast Asia,** leading to domestic development.

332. **Dutch culture also left a mark on modern Indonesian features, such as language.**

333. During their exploration, **the Dutch introduced Protestant Christianity to Indonesia.**

334. **The Dutch were among the first nations to convert to Protestant faiths during the Reformation,** so undertaking missionary activities was very important.

335. **Christians are an important minority in the country today,** though the majority of the Indonesian population is Muslim.

336. **The Dutch government, soon after realizing the potential of the colonial enterprise,** sponsored the creation a state-owned company to oversee the control and the inflow of trade from the Dutch East Indies.

337. **The United East Indies Company, or the Vereenigde Oost-Indische Compagnie (VOC),** was granted state charters that greatly increased its capabilities, making it essentially its own small functioning state with a developed bureaucracy.

338. For instance, in 1602, the **VOC was granted the right to wage wars and establish towns in the name of the Dutch government** in the Dutch East Indies.

339. In 1619, **the VOC established its base in what is now Jakarta, then known as Batavia,** where they could collect taxes from merchants trading with other countries throughout Asia and Africa.

340. **To ensure control over its new territories, the VOC imposed heavy taxation** on imported goods while forbidding Europeans from entering certain ports without permission.

341. **The company sought to monopolize the spice trade,** which was highly profitable during this era, by eliminating competition among traders operating within their borders.

342. **Over time, the Dutch gained almost complete control over Indonesia** and continued to journey farther into the Pacific to expand their colonies.

343. For instance, **Dutch explorer Jacob Roggeveen was the first documented European to make landfall on Easter Island** in 1722.

344. **Upon his arrival, he encountered the local Rapa Nui people,** who had developed their society while being secluded from the rest of the world.

345. By the 18th century, **the majority of Indonesia had become part of the Dutch East Indies.** The VOC had set up several forts throughout the region to protect their trading interests from foreign marauders.

346. By the mid-18th century, **instability created by wars, the emergence of competitors,** widespread corruption, and poor management led to the dissolution of the VOC.

347. **The Dutch established plantations to produce commodities such as coffee, sugarcane, and tea,** which could be sold back home at a high price.

348. **Dutch colonial activities expanded in the 19th century,** when European powers dominated international trade and set up colonies all around the world.

349. **During World War II, the Dutch East Indies were invaded by imperial Japan,** which took over the colony's valuable rubber and oil fields.

350. **According to UN estimates, up to four million people died in Dutch Indonesia due to Japanese occupation,** which lasted until 1945.

351. In 1949, **Indonesia gained full independence from Dutch rule** and is now one of the world's most populous democracies.

British Expansion in East Asia and India
(1600–1839)

For centuries, the British have had a presence in India and East Asia. This chapter will explore the history of their expansion during this period with seventeen interesting facts.

352. **In 1600, the East India Company was founded in England to trade spices from Asia and India.**

353. **The British had become interested in getting involved in the spice trade since the defeat of the Spanish-Portuguese armada in 1585,** which opened up new possibilities for Britain overseas.

354. **The company was formed by several prominent English merchants who managed to obtain a royal charter from Queen Elizabeth I,** gaining a fifteen-year monopoly in English trade in the East Indies.

355. **The East India Company traded with Java, Sumatra, Japan and other parts of Asia** for goods like silk, porcelain, tea, and spices.

356. **The East India Company eventually grew to become the world's largest trading company,** amounting to about a half of all of world's trade.

357. **By 1611, several ships had sailed from England to East Asia and India as part of Britain's growing global trade network.**

358. In 1604, **Captain Henry Middleton became one of the first Englishmen sent out by his country to explore India** and its people.

359. In 1608, **Captain William Hawkins arrived in Gujarat, India,** to establish trade relations between England and the Mughal Empire.

360. In 1619, **Britain established a trading post in Surat on India's west coast,** which became one of their first official colonies in the region.

361. By 1613, **more English traders were arriving who set up shop in Agra,** an important city for trading with Mughal Empire rulers at that time.

362. Although **the British East India Company** was not a major direct participant in the transatlantic slave trade, it did engage in the internal slave trade within the territories it controlled in India.

363. During its peak period of territorial expansion and control in the late 18th century, **the East India Company was involved in the practice of slavery and bonded labor,** primarily through its oversight and governance of local systems that included forms of servitude and forced labor.

364. **By the mid-17th century, the British had tried to set up trading posts in Southeast Asia,** though those would not become impactful until decades later.

365. In the 18th century, **with the rise of tea as the new hot commodity for European markets, the British began to increasingly trade with China,** financing their endeavors with illegal exports of opium to China.

366. **This ultimately led to the Opium Wars, a series of conflicts that began in 1839.** The wars were caused by the Chinese government's decision to prohibit the opium trade in the country and Britain's decision to continue smuggling opium into the country.

367. **Despite the fact that British possessions in India and Southeast Asia were ultimately contested by other European powers, such as France and the Netherlands,** Britain continued to expand its presence in the region throughout the 19th century.

368. **Indian and Southeast Asian trade would become an important part of the British economy,** only declining with the era of decolonization after World War II.

French Settlement in North America
(1608–1770)

Discover the intriguing history of French settlement in North America. Learn how they established their first permanent settlement and the efforts of Samuel de Champlain.

369. **In 1608, France established the first permanent European settlement in Canada.** The settlement was called Quebec City.

370. **The French settlers named their new territory New France.**

371. From 1608 to 1710, **French explorers claimed much of modern-day Canada and parts of the United States for France.**

372. **Samuel de Champlain was one of the most important figures** during this period. He is often called the **"Father of New France."**

373. **Champlain helped to create a government in New France.** He also explored much of eastern North America for settlements and trade opportunities with Native American tribes living there.

374. **New France included parts of modern-day Ontario, Quebec, Nova Scotia, and the Canadian Maritime provinces.**

375. **New France also reached south into the United States.** The French claimed regions in present-day **Louisiana** (which they called Louisiane, as well as parts of **Maine**, **Michigan**, and other regions west of **the Mississippi.**

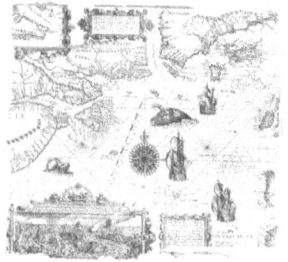

376. **Beaver furs were a profitable part of New France's economy.** The fur trade helped establish relations between the French and the Native Americans.

377. **The French settlers relied heavily on Native American tribes to help with farming and hunting** so they could survive in their new home environment.

378. **In 1703, King Louis XIV gave control of New France to Philippe de Rigaud,** Marquis of Vaudreuil, the former Governor of Montreal.

379. **Philippe de Rigaud was governor-general of New France** from 1703 until his death in 1725.

380. **During the rule of Governor-General Vaudreuil, the British Empire made many attempts to take over New France.** These efforts all failed.

381. **France's extensive colonial activities culminated in the French and Indian War** (1754–1763), which resulted in France giving up its claims to North America except for two small islands off Newfoundland.

382. In 1759, **British General James Wolfe defeated French General Louis Montcalm at the Battle of Quebec,** which was a major turning point in the French and Indian War.

383. By 1770, **most of the remaining French settlements had been ceded to either Britain or Spain.**

384. **French possessions in North America came to an end with the Louisiana Purchase in the early 19th century,** when **Emperor Napoleon** sold the Louisiana Territory to the United States.

385. **Although New France changed control about three centuries ago,** French language and customs remain prevalent in modern-day Canada, especially in Quebec.

Mayflower Lands at Plymouth
(1620)

This chapter will explore the significant history of Plymouth Colony. We'll look at intriguing facts about where the Mayflower arrived, why the Pilgrims set sail in the first place, and something called the Mayflower Compact.

386. In November 1620, **the Mayflower arrived in what is now Plymouth Harbor, Massachusetts.**

387. **The voyage was meant to end in the Colony of Virginia** but ended up northward due to poor weather and navigational challenges.

388. **Aboard the ship were Pilgrims from the Church of England,** who had left Britain due to religious differences with the Church's doctrine.

389. **Accounts state that 102 people were on board the Mayflower.** Although the ship is best known for the Pilgrims who sought religious freedom, there were other people on board searching for a new life.

390. In November of 1620, **they signed an agreement called the Mayflower Compact** to create a peaceful and orderly government for their new colony.

391. **The Mayflower Compact also included provisions about religious tolerance** – an aspect instrumental for the later American Constitution.

392. **The document is thus considered the first written framework of government in the territories of the United States.**

393. In March 1621, **Massasoit, the leader of the Wampanoag tribe, and Governor William Bradford created a pact** that established a friendship between the two groups for several decades.

394. **The Pilgrims were able to sustain their colony mainly due to the help from Native Americans,** who gave them food and taught them how to survive.

395. **In the Spring of 1621, two advanced scouts named Squanto and Samoset** helped the settlers learn about their new surroundings and taught them how to cultivate native plants like corn.

396. In the fall of 1621, **Governor William Bradford organized the first Thanksgiving in America,** with Massasoit and some of his men joining the English for dinner.

397. **In 1630, the population at Plymouth Colony had grown significantly,** largely because of the influx of European immigrants arriving after having learned about the religious freedom and economic opportunities there.

398. By this time, **there were established trade routes between the Plymouth Colony and Jamestown,** although trade did not take place on a large scale.

399. In 1691, **Plymouth Colony joined the Massachusetts Bay Colony.**

400. Remnants of the original **Plymouth Colony** are now a living history museum known as **Plimoth Patuxet Museums.**

401. Due to its unique history as one of the first colonial endeavors to embody the spirit of the United States, **the establishment of Plymouth after the Mayflower expedition is still revered as an iconic symbol.**

Dutch Exploration of South Africa
(1650–1800)

This chapter will explore the Dutch exploration of South Africa between 1650 and 1800. We'll uncover fifteen fascinating facts about this period, such as what settlements were created and conflicts that took place.

402. **Dutch settlers first arrived in South Africa in the mid-1600s,** creating a permanent settlement in 1652 at **Cape Town.**

403. **The Dutch East India Company was granted permission by the Netherlands to explore areas around Cape Town** that had been explored earlier by Portuguese sailors.

404. In 1652, **Jan van Riebeeck set up a base at Table Bay,** where he began to build **Fort de Goede Hoop** (Fort Good Hope).

405. **This fort became an important trading post for ships sailing between Europe and Asia** during this period. It would eventually be replaced by the Castle of Good Hope, which is still standing.

406. **Van Riebeeck and other settlers** cultivated vegetables like cabbage and carrots.

407. **Ships relied on salted meat and dried fish for sustenance,** but they took fresh food from **Cape Town** on their long journeys, which helped prevent scurvy.

408. **The town of Stellenbosch was founded in 1679 by Governor Simon van der Stel,** who named it after himself.

409. **Over the centuries, this region has become known for its wine production thanks to its favorable climate and earth conditions.** Wine continues to be made in this region today.

410. In the late 17th century, **a group of Huguenots (French Protestants) fleeing religious persecution in France settled in Cape Town and brought with them skills in winemaking,** contributing to the growth of the wine industry in the region.

411. The Cape Colony slowly became dominated by the VOC, emerging as the company's governorate until 1795.

412. However, the philosophy of the VOC, whose activities were centered around extracting profit from the East Indies, came into direct conflict with the situation at the Cape Colony, which became an attractive place for Dutch settlers.

413. The city of Swellendam was founded by Dutch settlers in 1745; it is now one of South Africa's oldest towns and still has many original colonial buildings from the 1700s standing today.

414. During this time, many wars broke out between local indigenous groups around Cape Town due to disputes over land rights or resources. These conflicts had long-lasting impacts on the natives.

415. By 1800, **almost all of the indigenous Khoikhoi tribes in the Cape had been severely impacted by European settlers.** Diseases, conflict, and the loss of their land greatly affected their way of life.

416. Dutch settlers in South Africa introduced their own language, which would evolve into the modern Afrikaans language, one of the most widespread languages in Africa.

French and British Colonization of Mauritius Island
(1715-1968)

This chapter will explore the long and complex history of French and British colonization on Mauritius Island. We'll uncover interesting facts about the successive French and British settlements on this island.

417. **The French took control of Mauritius in 1715, naming it Isle de France** after the Dutch abandoned it.

418. **Mauritius was valuable to the French as a stopover on the route to the East Indies,** serving as a replenishment point for ships traveling the Indian Ocean.

419. **The island was administered by the French East India Company,** which developed the island's infrastructure and agricultural base, particularly in sugar production.

420. **Slavery was integral to the island's economy under French rule,** with slaves being brought from Africa, Madagascar, and the Indian subcontinent to work on the sugar plantations.

421. **As governor, Mahé de Labourdonnais is credited with transforming Mauritius into a prosperous colony,** improving infrastructure like roads and buildings, including the famous Château de Mon Plaisir at Pamplemousses.

422. **Named the capital in 1735 by Labourdonnais, Port Louis** became a major naval base and shipbuilding center.

423. **The British captured Mauritius from the French during the Napoleonic Wars,** largely due to its strategic position in the Indian Ocean.

424. **Slavery was abolished under British rule in 1835,** leading to labor shortages, which were filled by indentured laborers from India.

425. **The introduction of indentured labor from India changed the demographic and cultural landscape of Mauritius,** with Indian culture influencing various aspects of life, including cuisine and religion.

426. **Under British rule, the economy of Mauritius became heavily reliant on sugar production,** which remained a key export throughout the colonial period.

427. **The establishment of railways by the British improved the transportation of goods and people across the island,** boosting economic activities.

428. **The botanical gardens in Pamplemousses, initiated by Labourdonnais,** became famous for their collection of indigenous and exotic plants.

429. **During World War II, Mauritius served as a refuge for evacuees from the Seychelles** and a base for military operations against Axis powers in the Indian Ocean.

430. **Mauritius became an independent nation on March 12th, 1968,** following a period of increased push for self-governance fueled by the global decolonization movement.

Russian Exploration of the Aleutian Islands
(1670–1679)

As the history of the Age of Exploration continues to fascinate us, so does the story of the Russian exploration of the Aleutian Islands. This chapter will explore over twenty interesting facts about their journeys to the Aleutian Islands.

431. In the late 17th century, **Russian explorers began to show interest in the Pacific region,** beginning their exploration of Alaska and the neighboring islands.

432. **Russia is not always remembered for its overseas colonial legacies,** though its control over Alaska constituted one of the most intriguing parts of North American early modern history.

433. **In addition to Alaska, Russians would also establish a temporary presence at Fortress Ross, California, in 1812,** which would last until 1841.

434. **Headed by explorers Vitus Bering and Aleksei Chirikov,** the Russians made landfall in Alaska.

435. **The strait between Alaska and Russia, the Bering Strait,** thus bears the name of the first explorer to effectively cross it by sea.

436. **The primary incentive for exploring this area was obtaining furs from the animals who called the islands home.** Sea otters and fur seals were highly prized.

437. **At that time, the main inhabitants of the region were indigenous natives,** with whom the Russians established trade relations.

438. **They were successful in finding different furry animals,** which they hunted extensively in order to trade their furs in different markets.

439. **Overhunting led to ecological issues and impacted the indigenous people's livelihoods.**

440. In addition to setting up trading posts, **the Russians also brought with them Christian missionaries who spread Eastern Orthodox Christianity to Alaskan natives.**

441. **This was one of the first instances of concentrated missionary activities in North America** on behalf of the Eastern Orthodox Church.

442. By the late 18th century, **it became clear that Russia could not maintain effective control over the colony in the long term,** as it was greatly unprofitable when Russian efforts to colonize and trade were decentralized.

443. **This prompted Russian traders to ask for government support and set up a comprehensive fur trade system in 1799,** known as the Russian American Company.

444. **Throughout its existence, the Russian American Company became a rather successful endeavor,** even funding the first Russian circumnavigation of the world in 1803.

445. **The Russian American Company had its headquarters in the city of New Archangelsk,** the modern-day **city of Sitka, Alaska.**

446. In 1867, **the Russian government sold modern-day Alaska to the United States for a little over seven million dollars.** The Russian American Company's commercial interests were sold off.

447. **Russian settlers cataloged and studied local plant and animal life,** as well as the customs of the native people living on these islands, during this period.

448. **Russians introduced foxes to the Aleutian Islands and parts of Alaska in hopes of establishing a new source of income from their furs.**

449. **Russian sailors also ventured to mainland Alaska,** where they encountered the indigenous Tlingit and Haida people.

450. **However, they never really founded any significant settlements inland**. Instead, they chose to stay near the coast and develop existing posts and relationships with the natives.

451. **They often forced the native populations into serfdom,** exploiting their labor for their own designs.

British Exploration of the Pacific Northwest Coast
(1791–the mid-1800s)

Discover fifteen fascinating facts about the British exploration of the Pacific Northwest, such as famous explorers and competitors for the region.

452. In 1791, **British explorer George Vancouver set sail from England with two ships to explore the Pacific Northwest coast of North America.**

453. **Vancouver's crew was made up of officers, sailors, and scientists** who were looking for trading opportunities and to map new territories for Britain.

454. **Vancouver and his crew set off on their journey from the San Francisco area northward toward British Columbia,** mapping one of the most hard-to-explore territories in North America.

455. **Vancouver continued his expedition by mapping out what is now known as British Columbia, Washington State, and southeast Alaska** between 1792 and 1794.

456. **When he returned home, he brought with him many charts of the newly discovered areas,** which were published after his death.

457. Today, **the city of Vancouver and Vancouver Island are named after the British explorer.**

458. **Other nations besides Great Britain had tried to explore the Pacific Northwest before Vancouver's expedition, most notably the Spanish.**

459. **The 1774 expedition, sponsored by the new viceroy of New Spain and headed by Juan Perez,** reached the Queen Charlotte Islands in July of the same year.

460. **The Spanish sent another expedition a year later, mapping the coastline and the immediate areas near it.** The region seemed attractive because it was so vast and mysterious.

461. In the late 1780s, **Spanish explorers reached Nootka Sound on Vancouver Island.** Their presence led to an outbreak of tensions between them, the British, and the native population of Vancouver.

462. **The incident, known as the Nootka Crisis, nearly brought Britain and Spain into war over trade rights in the region.** The tensions were ultimately resolved through peaceful means, with merchants from both nations being able to trade.

463. **Another British explorer, John Meares,** arrived on the Pacific Northwest coast looking for trading opportunities with Asia and charting out new territories for Britain.

464. By the late 18th century, **countries from all over Europe were competing to explore and take control of different regions of the Pacific Northwest.**

465. **The interest in the region was increased after the discovery of gold in the western United States and Alaska, which led to a gold rush.**

466. **This resulted in additional exploratory activities** that increased the growth of the region and produced further disputes between interested parties.

Exploration of Australia, New Zealand, and the Antarctic
(1600s–1911)

This chapter will take us back to the "latest stage" of the European Age of Discovery— the exploration of the Antarctic and the Australasian region. After the late 1600s, the focus of European exploration shifted toward this region, leading to many fascinating discoveries that shaped our understanding of the continents of Australia and Antarctica.

467. **The "mythical" South Land, Terra Australis, was sought by many European navigators,** influencing the exploration of the Southern Hemisphere.

468. In 1606, **the first recorded European sighting of Australia was made by Dutch navigator Willem Janszoon aboard the Duyfken.**

469. In 1642, **Abel Tasman, another Dutch explorer, became the first European to sight New Zealand and later Tasmania,** which he named **Van Diemen's Land.**

470. **Abel Tasman's voyage led to the first European encounter with Māori in New Zealand.**

471. **The introduction of European diseases had devastating impacts on indigenous populations** in Australia and New Zealand.

472. **William Dampier, an English buccaneer and navigator,** landed on the northwest coast of Australia in 1688, the first Englishman to set foot on Australian soil.

473. **Captain James Cook's first voyage, which lasted from 1768 to 1771,** included mapping the entire coast of **New Zealand** and **the east coast of Australia,** claiming the latter for Britain.

474. **Cook's second voyage involved crossing the Antarctic Circle for the first time in recorded history.**

475. On his third voyage in 1777, **Cook returned to the Pacific,** further exploring the Polynesian islands.

476. In 1788, **the First Fleet arrived in Botany Bay,** marking the beginning of British penal settlements in Australia.

477. In 1824, **the British formally claimed possession of the whole of Australia as New South Wales.**

478. **George Vancouver explored the southwest coast of Australia in 1791,** further detailing the continent's coastline.

479. From 1797 to 1798, **George Bass and Matthew Flinders proved that Tasmania was an island** by circumnavigating it.

480. **Matthew Flinders's voyage** on the Investigator was the first to circumnavigate Australia and identify it as a continent.

481. **Charles Darwin visited New Zealand and Australia in 1835 and 1836,** offering critical scientific observations on the geology and biology of the region.

482. IN 1873, **the HMS Challenger explored deep-sea trenches near New Zealand,** expanding knowledge of marine biology.

483. **William Smith discovered the South Shetland Islands in 1819,** initiating the era of Antarctic exploration.

484. **In 1820, Fabian Gottlieb von Bellingshausen, a Russian explorer,** saw the Antarctic mainland.

485. In the early 1830s, **James Clark Ross conducted magnetic surveys** in the Antarctic and around Australia and New Zealand.

486. **Charles Wilkes led the United States Exploring Expedition to the Antarctic** in 1840, claiming a portion of the continent for America.

487. **In 1841, James Clark Ross discovered the Ross Sea and Ross Ice Shelf.**

488. **The discovery of gold in New South Wales and Victoria in 1851 led to the Australian Gold Rush,** significantly increasing the population.

489. In the 1890s, **gold was discovered in western Australia, leading to a second gold rush** that further spurred the development and population growth in the region.

490. **The 1860s saw numerous expeditions explore the interior of Australia,** revealing the harsh and varied landscapes.

491. **The Challenger expedition of 1872–1876, a global scientific voyage, conducted extensive oceanographic research around Australia, New Zealand, and the deep Southern Ocean.**

492. **The first International Polar Year in 1882** was a cooperative effort focused on meteorological and geophysical phenomena in polar areas.

493. **Carsten Borchgrevink claimed to be the first to set foot on the Antarctic mainland at Cape Adare** in 1895.

494. In 1899, **the British Antarctic Expedition, led by Carsten Borchgrevink,** was the first to winter on the Antarctic continent.

495. **The Discovery expedition, led by Robert Falcon Scott, carried out scientific and exploration work in Antarctica** from 1901 to 1904.

496. **Ernest Shackleton's Nimrod expedition reached a new farthest south record;** he was only ninety-seven miles from the South Pole.

497. In 1908, **Douglas Mawson, an Australian geologist,** explored large areas of the Antarctic coastline.

498. **Robert Falcon Scott's ill-fated Terra Nova expedition reached the South Pole,** but tragically, all members of the party died on the return journey.

499. In 1911, **Roald Amundsen of Norway reached the South Pole,** beating Scott and marking the first successful expedition to do so.

500. In 1953, **Sir Edmund Hillary from New Zealand, along with Tenzing Norgay,** became famous for their conquest of **Mount Everest**, but Hillary was also pivotal in Antarctic expeditions during the mid-20th century.

Conclusion

The past five centuries have seen unparalleled exploration and expansion by European powers. From **Christopher Columbus's** voyage to the Americas, **Portuguese explorations of Africa, India, and Brazil, the Spanish colonization of Mexico and Central and South America,** and **Captain James Cook's journey to New Zealand,** this book has explored some of **Europe's greatest voyages** from 1415 to 1800.

From privateering on open seas to English colonization in North America, these stories are evidence that **Europeans were determined conquerors with big dreams for large territories,** even if that came at the expense of those already living there.

If you enjoyed this book, a review on Amazon would be greatly appreciated because it would mean a lot to hear from you.

To leave a review:

1. Open your camera app.
2. Point your mobile device at the QR code.
3. The review page will appear in your web browser.

Thanks for your support!

Check out another book in the series

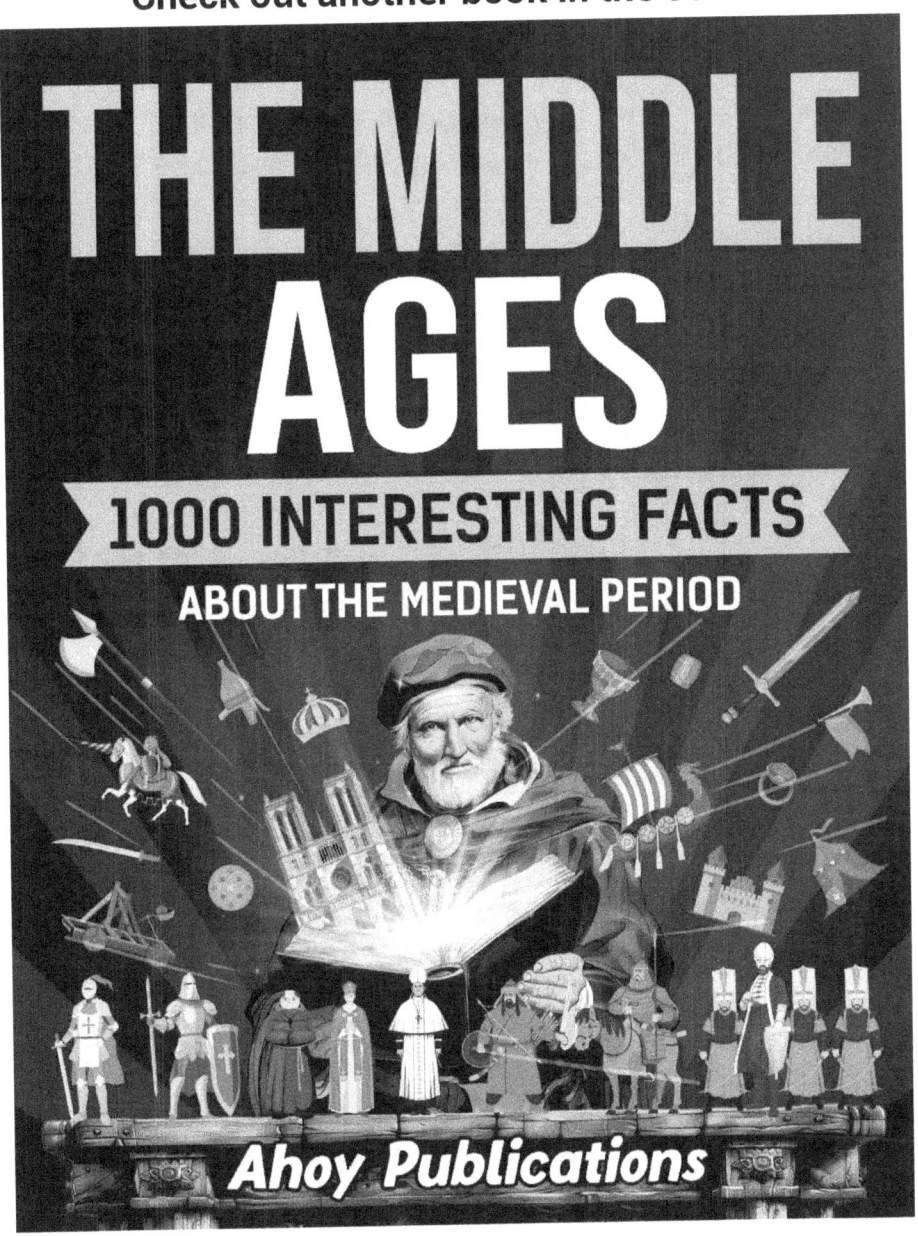

Welcome Aboard, Check Out This Limited-Time Free Bonus!

Ahoy, reader! Welcome to the Ahoy Publications family, and thanks for snagging a copy of this book! Since you've chosen to join us on this journey, we'd like to offer you something special.

Check out the link below for a FREE e-book filled with delightful facts about American History.

But that's not all - you'll also have access to our exclusive email list with even more free e-books and insider knowledge. Well, what are ye waiting for? Click the link below to join and set sail toward exciting adventures in American History.

Access your bonus here: https://ahoypublications.com/

Or, Scan the QR code!

Sources and Additional References

"Exploration of Africa." Worldhistory.org, 2020, https://worldhistory.org/exploration-of-africa/.

"Prince Henry the Navigator." Encyclopedia Britannica, Encyclopedia Britannica, Inc., 26 June 2019, https://www.britannica.com/biography/Prince-Henry-the-Navigator.

Cohen, Jeffrey. "Christopher Columbus: Biography and Accomplishments." Encyclopedia Britannica, 20 May 2020, https://www.britannica.com/biography/Christopher-Columbus.

"Christopher Columbus." History, A&E Television Networks, history.com/topics/exploration/christopher-columbus.

"Portuguese India." Encyclopedia Britannica, Encyclopedia Britannica, Inc., 22 Jan. 2021, www.britannica.com/place/Portuguese-India.

Elliott, J. H. Imperial Spain 1469-1716. Penguin Books, 2003.

"Early European Exploration: The Spanish Conquistadors." National Geographic Society, 22 June 2018, www.nationalgeographic.org/encyclopedia/early-european-exploration-the-spanish-conquistadors/.

Crampton, Julia. "Ferdinand Magellan." Biography.com, A&E Television Networks, 8 Sept. 2020, www.biography.com/explorer/ferdinand-magellan

Franklin, Rachel. "The Spice Islands: History & Meaning." History.com, A&E Television Networks, 9 Apr. 2019, www.history.com/topics/exploration/spice-islands

"Hernán Cortés' Conquest of Mexico." History.com, A&E Television Networks, 8 July 2019, www.history.com/topics/exploration/hernan-cortes-conquest-of-mexico.

Solano, Matias. "The Spanish Conquest of Peru: Francisco Pizarro," Ancient History Encyclopedia, 4 Mar. 2021, https://www.ancient.eu/Pizarro_Franci/

"Jacques Cartier and Exploration of Canada." CanadaHistory.ca, www.canadahistory.com/sections/Exploration/JacquesCartier.html.

"Jesuit Missions in Latin America | History | Smithsonian Magazine." Smithsonian Magazine, Smithsonian Institution, 20 Dec. 2017, www.smithsonianmag.com/history/jesuit-missions-in-latin-america-1213521/.

Shaw, Earle. "The Legacy of Spanish Rule in the Philippines." Research Gate, www.researchgate.net/publication/316631946_The_Legacy_of_Spanish_Rule_in_the_Philippines.

"The Jamestown Colony." Jamestown-Yorktown Foundation, Jamestown-Yorktown Foundation, 2020, jamestownyorktown.org/jamestown-story/jamestown-colony/.

Steel, Ronald. "The Dutch Legacy in Indonesia." History.com, A&E Television Networks, 10 June 2011, https://www.history.com/news/the-dutch-legacy-in-indonesia.

MacDougall, Eliza. "British Expansion in the 16th & 17th Centuries." 16th & 17th Century British Expansion, Scholarly Commons, digitalcommons.conncoll.edu/cgi/viewcontent.cgi?article=1164&context=historystudentprojects.

"The Massachusetts Bay Colony." Plimoth Plantation, 2020, www.plimoth.org/learn/just-kids/homework-help/massachusetts-bay-colony.

"Mauritius." Britannica, The Editors of Encyclopedia Britannica, https://www.britannica.com/place/Mauritius-island-Indian-Ocean.

"British Exploration of the Pacific Northwest." University of Oregon. Accessed April 13, 2021. https://uoregon.edu/~rludeke/GeoNotebook/Ch%20Elliottbay/britishesp.html.